Foreword

Memories of Bury is a compilation of photographs from the not-too-distant past, chosen according to their ability to rekindle memories of days gone by. The pictures on the following pages should be within the memory of the majority of our readers, setting the book apart from the worthy, but different works of local history that are available.

Our aim is to provide a catalyst capable of evoking feelings of nostalgia in anyone with an interest in Bury, rather than to write a history of the area in 'text-book' style. This modest book has more to do with entertainment than serious study, but we hope it is none the worse for that!

The following pages contain a variety of pictures charting local places and events, covering happy times and sad, along with sporting milestones and many of the places you would expect to visit on a nostalgic tour of Bury. We hope that people with a genuine interest in the town will be prompted to recall the distinctive sights, sounds and even aromas associated with the Bury of the recent past, and if this is the outcome we will have achieved our aim.

Compiling *Memories of Bury* has been a pleasure. Whatever your age, we hope you enjoy reading it. Happy memories!

Above: Kay Gardens provides a relaxing haven for weary shoppers in this 1956 photograph

Mark Smith and Phil Holland
True North Books

First published in 1997 by:
True North Books
Dean Clough
Halifax
HX3 5AX
Tel 01422 344344

a true north book

Copyright: © True North Holdings
ISBN: 1 900 463 90 3

£4.99 nett

Contents

Above: A sea of faces fill this raised view of Bury's open market, taken in 1968.

Acknowledgments

The publishers would like to thank the following for helping to make this book possible: The staff of Bury Central Library, in particular Alan Boughey and Penney Farrell of the Reference and Information section who kindly allowed us to reproduce around forty pictures from their collection. Thanks are also due to Eric Bentley who provided several pictures of trains, Clifford C Ashton, who supplied the spectacular photographs of fire scenes, Peter Cullen for providing help with captions and photographs of Bury Football Club, and Chris Gribben who supplied several pictures of the old Market Hall. The publishers are also grateful to the local companies who have supported this book and allowed us to relate their often fascinating histories. Finally, many thanks to Andrew Hales for organising the inclusion of local businesses and to Mandy Walker for bringing her desktop publishing expertise to these pages.

A commemorative picture of the interior of James Kenyon and Son, cotton spinners and manufacturers, among many other activities. The company had several mill properties throughout the district and were major local employers as well as serious players in the cotton industry. The company can trace its roots back to 1714, making it not only one of the oldest cotton enterprises in the north, but one of the earliest commercial businesses of any description in Britain! These hard working ladies represent several generations and no doubt each would have a fascinating story to tell about life as they had experienced it. Gone are the days when young girls could get a job in the mill, perhaps besides her mother or sisters, and expect to keep it until marriage, children or retirement would interrupt it.

Another picture from James Kenyon and Son Ltd., showing white-coated ladies in rather spartan working conditions in 1953. Kenyon's was originally founded in Crimble, nearly three centuries ago. The move to Bury involved acquiring premises at Derby Street. The 'Son' in the title of the firm was originally Richard Kenyon, the son of the founder. Richard and his father were commissioners in the Bury Improvement Commission, a very worthy organisation set up to look at many different aspects of ordinary working people's lives with the aim of achieving fundamental improvements. Tragically Richard was killed in an accident at the age of just thirty years. Another son, James, was a major force in the business who went on to become Bury's Member of Parliament. He was later honoured for his work by being made a Freeman of the Borough.

Mill working has been central to the lives of countless thousands of Bury people for generations. The picture here is of the interior of one of James Kenyon and Son's mills but it is representative of the scores of similar businesses which could be found within a few miles of the centre of Bury. Cotton production and processing has seen its ups and downs over the last century; the extremes of wealth and hardship have been associated with the industry, and this is reflected in things such as the state of the massive buildings where the work is carried out, as well as the generous donations of parks, libraries and public buildings made possible during the times of plenty. Foreign imports have traditionally been blamed for some of the more difficult times in the cotton trade, a point made very strongly to Ghandhi when he visited Lancashire in 1931.

Left: Bright sunshine graced the day in 1955 when the Mayor, his wife and other local officials took the salute in Market Place for one of the first official engagements of the new Mayor of Bury.

Councillor Joseph Birks, seen here with his wife, Mrs J Birks, was one of the most popular Mayors that Bury had had. The ceremony to confirm his appointment to office took place in the Town Hall Chambers on May 25 1955, witnessed by other councillors and officials, along with many of his friends and supporters. Cllr Birks was a one time sportsman, trade unionist and magistrate; he took on the role of Mayor at the age of 58. During an emotional and inspiring speech Cllr Birks, a lifelong Labour activist, described his programme of plans for his time in office. Improving local schools was the main priority, the building of a new bus station and upgrading the area's street lighting would soon begin, and, in common with virtually every other town in post-war Britain, a programme of housing improvements would be embarked upon.

Right: Nineteen-fifty-three was the date this picture was taken at Warth Mills. The occasion was the Coronation of Her Majesty Queen Elizabeth II, one which caused tremendous celebration throughout the whole of Britain. This was one of the first national events to really capture the hearts and minds of ordinary people since the misery they endured throughout the war years.

Warth Mill was formerly Mellor's Mill and had a long association with the cotton industry. The mill was constructed by Colonel John James Mellor, the youngest of 15 children, in the 1860s. The importance of Mellor's contribution to Bury life was such that Mellor Hall and Mellor Street were named after him. During the Second World War the government requisitioned the property for use as a wartime prison, housing German and Italian prisoners. After the war the mill was involved in the cotton industry for a short time, and was later taken over and operated by Macpherson's paints.

In 1936 it was decided to hold a competition to secure the best possible design for a new town hall for Bury. The contest was won by the architect Reginald Edmonds, and his clean, modern, not to say functional design was adopted. The building was steel-framed and used Stancliffe stone in its construction. The chosen site was land between Knowsley Street and Manchester Road, just a stone's throw from the town centre. Work began in 1938, and the foundation stone was laid by the Earl of Derby on 14 April 1939. By 1940 the main shell of the building was completed, but the citizens of Bury, in common with people throughout the rest of the country had other things on their mind by now. Wartime meant that work had to be suspended, and the half-finished building took on the role of the headquarters of the local Air Raid Precautions (ARP) unit. 1947 saw the resumption of building work, the building was constructed with flexibility of use in mind, an advanced concept at this time. The building was noted for its simple dignity and clean modern lines - all features which have stood the test of time. Rhodesian teak flooring and a mahogany-framed council chamber were incorporated into the design which generally met with widespread approval. Bury people were delighted and honoured by the Queen's agreement to formally open the Town Hall and they turned out to welcome her in their thousands.

This picture dates from just after the end of the First World War. It was taken in the Walmsley Road area of Bury and shows workmen laying the tram tracks for the section from Limefield to the New Inn. There are a number of interesting features in the picture, including the very heavily-laden telegraph poles and the wooden wheelbarrows on the left of the picture. Steam powered trams had been around in Bury since 1883, and electric trams had been employed since 1903. The earliest form of popular public transport on the roads of Bury took the form of horse-drawn trams. Less than ten years after this scene was captured the end of the tramway era was heralded by the introduction of motorbuses. The year was 1925, and they were initially used on the route between Bury and Walshaw. By 1933 the Corporation had decided to phase out trams altogether, but the advent of the Second World War meant that transport matters assumed less priority, and so trams clung on until 1949.

This picture of Bolton Road, Bury Bridge prompts thoughts and memories of the major changes and improvements which took place along this stretch of road over the last few decades. Most people would agree that Bury Bridge used to be the town's most notorious bottleneck, and a talking point and major headache for local people for many years. This photograph dates from 1955 and features two young men involved in some kind of traffic census. Perhaps their work helped convince *the powers that be* of the need to take radical steps to cope with the volumes of traffic here. The first scheme was completed in August 1967 costing £40,000. In 1978 a £2 million scheme finally solved the problem.

In 1846, Joseph Webb, a craftsman skilled in the art of manufacturing and rolling iron, based in the Staffordshire area, was drawn to the Bury area by the demand from the burgeoning cotton industry for rolled iron bars and other metal products. Webb founded a small rolling mill, at the age of 44, alongside the established Soho foundry. The business grew and prospered, as did the Webb family of ten children. The last of his offspring, Henry and George, took over the running of the firm on the death of their father. Henry Webb was to go on to become a J.P, and was instrumental in the founding of Bury Girls Grammar School. He was a devout Methodist, and was the organist at New Road Chapel for 40 years. The Webb story is fascinating. George Webb went on to establish coffee houses in Lancashire and beyond after establishing the Bury Coffee House Company. Three of these fashionable meeting places were based in Bury, the most central, and best known of them being in Market Street. The early 1920s saw the closure of the rolling mill, though other aspects of the engineering business continued. Throughout the history of the firm it remained in the control of the Webb family. It continued until the death of William Webb in 1970.

Right: Union Street was the location of the shop and workshop pictured here. In the 1936 Bury Business Directory (a fascinating publication which listed every street and the head of each household or name of the business operating from the property) it states that the firm was run by W & T Avery. In the same directory (which is worth looking up, in the Reference Section of the Bury Central Library) businesses such as Amy Beetson's dressmakers and The Pineapple Inn are also listed as being on this street. The weighing scale industry had a great importance in the days before pre-packed foods, as every shop would have to weigh out almost everything that was purchased as it was bought. Shopping was therefore a more time consuming, personal and, some would say, more pleasurable activity than it is today.

Below: A promotional photograph of the interior of the Town Hall which dates from just a few years after it was taken. There is evidence here of the plain interior styling; functional, not ostentatious, as those responsible for the design would have explained. We should remember that in the decade after the end of the Second War all resources were in short supply. What there was tended to be expensive, and the rate payers of Bury would not have thanked their Councillors for wasting money on fripperies.

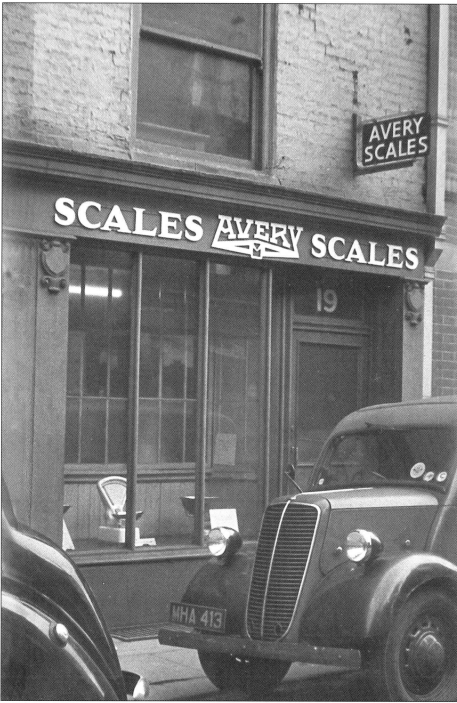

Newtons of Bury - traditional house furnishers for almost a century

The early days

There is a wealth of fascinating history behind the well known quality furniture business known as Newton's of Bury. The business was founded almost a century ago, in the year 1900, by Walter Newton. As trade grew Walter's son, Cyril assisted his father in the firm and set about learning every aspect of the job. As the dark days of the war arrived Cyril joined the Royal Navy and left to serve his country for the duration.

The business was originally based at Eccles, and this was its home for many years. Soon after Cyril returned from his war service the decision was taken to move the business to Bury, and a suitable location was soon found on Spring Street in the town. This served the business well for around 15 years, and the firm built upon its reputation for selling quality secondhand furniture and antiques. By this time *Newton's* was joined by Colin and Mavis Newton, the third generation of the family firm to be involved in the business.

The business prospered for the next 30 years, despite the ups and downs of the economy and the changing tastes which characterised this period. A major milestone was passed in 1992 when the ownership of the business passed into the hands of Glenn and Christine Wild. The Wild's were not newcomers to the firm, indeed Glenn Wild had already served 35 years at the company where he learned his trade as an expert French Polisher and Furniture Restorer. Christine Wild heads the busy manufacturing side of the business which involves the production of custom-made table protectors, 'Wild's Table Felts' which are in great demand from department stores, furniture shops and boardrooms for corporate clients throughout the country.

Diversity

By far the most important aspect of the business is still the supply of quality furnishings throughout the Lancashire area. This is supplemented by other services which include expert furniture restoration, french polishing and a re-upholstery service. All these services are carried out in the firm's own workshops which are situated locally.

Georgian House

Deceptive from the outside, many Bury folk and regular customers are aware of the internal size of Newton's store. However, many strangers, amazed by the three storeys inside the building have described the store as an 'Aladdin's Cave'. The building dates from 1780 and was formerly a private Georgian house. Visitors to the main showroom and workshops of Newton's of Bury cannot fail to be impressed by the unrivalled displays of top quality modern and traditional furniture which blend beautifully with the fine selection of antiques and collectors' items on show. The company is a leading stockist for some of the oldest and most respected reproduction and modern furniture manufacturers in the world, including Old Charm, Barr, Bridgecraft, Nathan, Rossmore, Strongbow and Reprodux. The selection of solid English oak furniture attracts buyers from all over England. Smaller collectors' items on show include Moorcroft pottery, period lamps, pictures and mirrors, reproduction radios and even world-renowned Steiff classic teddy bears! Newtons' excellent reputation for french polishing, upholstery and furniture restoration has led to commissions and contracts from all over the north of England.

Pride

Over the years generations of the same local families have returned again and again to Newton's of Bury for their furnishing requirements; a source of pride to the current proprietors, Glenn and Christine Wild. The owners have a strong belief in customer loyalty, support for the store and for Bury itself and are working hard to achieve this.

Above: An inside view of Newton's store showing the diversity of the products sold by the company.
Facing Page: Two views of The Rock dating from the early 1950s. On the large picture Newtons' store is now situated centre right.
Left: A turn of the century photograph of The Rock, illustrating the considerable work that was involved in laying tram lines on the main street, looking towards what is now the store, from the Black Bull.

Ernest Platt (Bury) Ltd - quality service for over 150 years

Above: William Platt, the founder's son, who was a government consultant on pensions and insurances.

Early history

The company now known as Ernest Platt (Bury) Ltd was established in the mid 1800s as a rubber merchants and mill furnishers. William A Platt started his humble business from his home in Walmersley Road, with the company name being WA Platt & Son. William's skill in his field earned him, after a time, the nickname of 'India Rubber Bill'.

Soon, William began to expand and diversify his business, moving into the field of boiler/pipe and heat insulation, recognising the enormous potential of this move. He devised and manufactured his own insulation compounds in works behind his home, in Buckley Street. As all factories and mills at that time were steam driven this was a good period for this type of work.

In the late 1890s until the First World War, all ships in the country's Navy were also steam powered and WA Platt & Son gained a lucrative and highly sought after Admiralty Contract to design and install the boiler pipes and heating on the fleet.

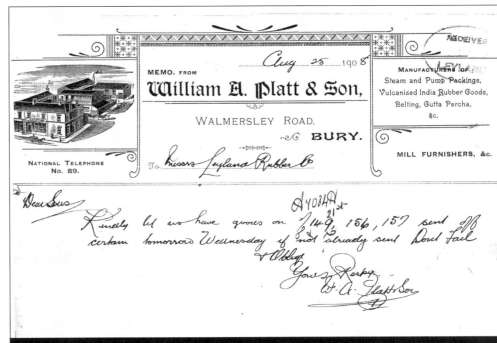

A letterhead dating from 1908, when the company was known as William A Platt & Son.

From wartime to an OBE.

The founder's son, also called William, was a councillor, JP and local church dignitary. A highly intelligent man, he helped with the War Savings Movement and was heavily involved with the Friendly Societies Movement. He was consulted by the Government, being an acknowledged authority on National Health, Insurance and Old Age Pensions, helping to set up the National Insurance Bill and later locally instigating the National Health Insurance act. For his work in this field he was awarded an MBE in 1912 and later OBE in 1932.

It was inevitable that because of all his Governmental work, William could not spend as much time on his company as he would have liked. Subsequently WA Platt & Son suffered, leading to 'downsizing' during the Depression, although the company continued to trade steadily through those years, doing much the same work.

William Platt died in 1933, leaving the business in the hands of his son, Ernest Alexander Platt. The business continued in the same vein throughout the

1940s and 1950s, doing many contractual insulation jobs in the late 1950s.

Time to diversify

1951 saw the death of Ernest Platt and the arrival of Wilfred Platt in the company. He formed a limited company in his father's name, Ernest Platt (Bury) Ltd and over the next two decades began to diversify the company, moving away from mill furnishings (as this was a time when the local mills were slowly dwindling) and boiler insulation. He geared the company more into the field of gasket manufacturing and sealing materials. This proved enormously successful but during the recession of the 1980s which led to the decline and closure of many local large factories and engineering works, Wilfred saw the need for expansion to broaden the company's outlook and customer base. With this in mind the company opened a branch in Blackburn in 1983.

Steady trading has continued ever since, with 1990 seeing the company move for the first time to its present site off Whalley Road, Shuttleworth, Ramsbottom, bringing the whole operation under one roof. There has been a steady expansion around gasket manufacturing and sealing material technology and the company now supplies a vast range of products for engineers.

Now in its fifth generation of the family, with Stephen Platt being the current Managing Director, Ernest Platt (Bury) Ltd has a very large local customer base and is also a contracted supplier to many major national companies. The company prides itself on the fact that it offers a first class service, perfected with years of experience and the ability to respond quickly to customer needs which are of prime importance.

Ernest Platt staff carrying out insulation work at East Lancashire Paper Mill at Radcliffe in 1955.

Excelsior - Over 100 years of specialist plastics processing

Excelsior was founded in 1896 by two Swedish businessmen to specialise in the manufacture of vulcanised fibre containers for the textile industry. By June 1902 the company was established at Greenend Works in Bacup and was trading as 'The Excelsior Fibre Co Ltd'.

Over the following decades Excelsior flourished with its extensive range of vulcanised fibre products which included doffing boxes and sliver cans

The Excelsior Fibre Co. Ltd.,
Greenend works
BACUP·LANCS.

(containers used in the textile industry) storage boxes, sample cases and attache cases all marketed under the 'Neverdone' trade name, chosen to emphasise the endless permutations of this versatile material and manufacturing process.

Fire!

Fire was a constant hazard and, in April 1946, Greenend Works was so badly damaged by a blaze that new premises had to be sought. So it was that 1946 saw the establishment of The Excelsior Fibre Co Ltd at a new location in Bury - Ferngrove Mills off Rochdale Old Road.

In 1952 the company was bought by the Fielding family, industrialists from Rochdale. Based at the Ferngrove Mill site the company continued to build on and develop the reputation of the 'Neverdone' fibreboard range of products until the 1970s when the decline of the textile industry encouraged a diversification of its product range. This decade, therefore, saw Excelsior move into rotational moulding (a form of plastics processing) with the development of its first plastic truck suitable for dye houses and laundries.

Name change

A whole range of other plastic materials handling products quickly followed suit. In 1979, to reflect its new, diversified product range, the company changed its name to Excelsior Containers (Bury) Ltd.

In 1984 Excelsior started to export and, soon, products manufactured in Bury were being exported all over Europe. By early 1987 Excelsior had acquired another rotational moulding plant, Smith Containers, based in Woolfold, Bury which was to become known as Smith Rotational Moulding Ltd. Excalibur Metal Products Ltd, located at the Bury Bridge Trading Estate was established in 1992 to manufacture sheet steel tooling used in the manufacture of rotationally moulded products and now exports its tooling and moulding machines all over the world. The company also acquired Crossfield Patterns Ltd., a Rochdale manufacturer of cast aluminium tooling in 1993. In 1994, when the production division of Excelsior Containers (Bury) Ltd, which had continued the manufacture of the traditional fibreboard products, albeit with the addition of many new product lines, materials and colours, moved to a newly refurbished site at Irwell

Works off Woodhill Road, Bury, offering increased production and storage space, it was decided to set up this side of the business once again as a separate autonomous company - Excelsior Case & Container Ltd.

The rotational moulding division was renamed Excelsior Rotational Moulding Ltd and remains at Ferngrove Mill, although after fifty years of continuous production by Excelsior at this site, it is hoped that this company will relocate to more modern premises in the near future.

Still locally based
1997 sees Excelsior Group International Limited* firmly established in the Bury area with four out of its five subsidiaries all manufacturing from sites within Bury.

* Established in the early 1990s as a holding organisation for the manufacturing companies.

Above left: An illustration taken from a brochure dating from the 1950s.

Facing page, left: The front cover of a brochure, advertising the 'Neverdone' range, dating from the early 1940s.

Facing page, right: This campaign ran from the 1950s, in the days when advertising on buses was just coming to the fore.

Below: The modern factory at Irwell Works, Lower Woodhill Road, Bury.

Senior Hargreaves - Celebrating 125 years of continued success in Bury

Henry Hargreaves, the founder of the firm, was born in 1851 in Ramsbottom, one of the seven children of a clogmaker. Henry Hargreaves 'served his time' with a local tinsmith in North Back King Street. Prior to 1890 a workshop was bought in Heywood Street. In these premises Henry's father made loaf tins to sell in the shop and in the Bury market at the weekends, along with grassboxes for lawnmowers. Henry

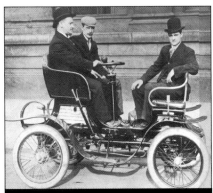

This vehicle (the first ever supplied in Bury) was purchased by Hargreaves & Sons for Cllr. Walter Ashworth in 1899

Hargreaves was a devout methodist and teetotaller. His devotion was taken to such an extent that he spurned the use of public transport on Sundays to walk to Ewood Bridge to preach; a distance of 14 miles.

Sovereigns

Henry was secretary to the choir, and one day, so the story goes, went on the annual choir trip, leaving his wife to feed the pigs. He had completely forgotten that he had hidden some golden sovereigns in the pigs' meal.

On returning home he asked his wife if she had fed the pigs. 'Yes' she replied, whereupon Henry informed her that she had fed the golden sovereigns to the pigs! As the money was needed to pay the expenses of the choir trip, Henry decided that the pigs must be killed. Out they went into the yard to do the deed, but providence was to intervene. It was a moon-lit night, and there, shining in the corner of the otherwise empty trough, were 13 shiny sovereigns, licked clean by the pigs!

Bicycle manufacturers

In 1892, premises were acquired in Silver Street. It was here that Henry Hargreaves and Sons began assembling and selling bicycles. All the family were involved in the bicycle and iron-mongery business. The works in Heywood Street were maintained, making principally grass boxes, and it was about this time that Hargreaves made their first roof ventilators, used on churches and schools.

Henry Hargreaves was responsible for introducing one of Bury's first motor cars. This vehicle, from the Royal Progress Works at Coventry, was acquired for Councillor Walter Ashworth, and the vehicle was displayed at the Manchester and District Cycle and Motor Show in 1899, of which Henry was Chairman. In 1905 the works known as Albert Works in Cook Street were acquired and from this point on the business became established in Cook Street. In 1903, the family left the premises in Silver Street to concentrate their efforts on Cook Street.

With the birth of the motor industry Henry Hargreaves sold the cycle business to concentrate wholly on sheet metal work. About this time Henry Hargreaves and Sons became firmly established, with Henry as managing director, James as foreman.

During the 1920s the Hargreaves business began to concentrate on the manufacture of ventilators and roof turrets. Some with ornamental designs fashioned from copper still grace many buildings today.

In 1931 Harry, by then Alderman Hargreaves died,

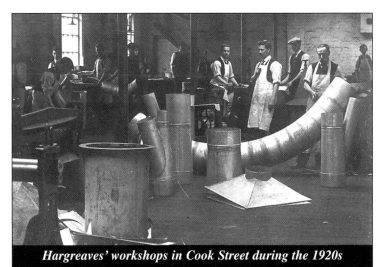

Hargreaves' workshops in Cook Street during the 1920s

and the business was then jointly run by his surviving sons, Robert and Harry until the death of Robert in 1940. From his home in St. Annes, where he lived between 1918 and 1939, Robert established many contacts in the Fylde area, with Blackpool as a particular centre of Hargreaves activities. Ventilation work was carried out in well-known buildings including the Tower; Winter Gardens; The Manchester Hotel; Cliffs Hotel; Savoy Hotel; Palace St.Annes; The Miners' Home Bispham; the Co-operative Emporium; the Oxford Cinema and innumerable churches and schools.

War years

In 1934 Hargreaves became a private limited company, and after Robert's death in 1940 Harry ran the business through the war years. In 1936 a future managing director, Henry Gordon Hargreaves, joined the firm as a draughtsman after leaving Bury Grammar School, and, at the same time, so did Joseph Bleakley, a future financial director.

The post war years have seen exciting times at Hargreaves with many major projects undertaken in the UK, ranging from nuclear power projects at most of Britain's nuclear facilities, to large manufacturing plants at Ford, Vauxhall, ICI and other major organisations. In 1946 the company employed 16 people and its only form of transport was a handcart! The growth in business soon resulted in the need for a dedicated transport fleet. Over the years the light green, eau de nil lorries, with maroon lettering were a familiar sight in many parts of the British Isles.

In 1953, Hargreaves acquired a plot of land on the other side of Cook Street from the California Engineering Company. This was the first foothold in

This picture dates from 1955 and shows the impressive fleet owned by the company at the time

a site now owned completely by Hargreaves, and one which played a major part in their development. In 1956, Hargreaves acquired even more land, a 12 acre site at Chamber Hall, adjoining Peel Mills, with the object of future expansion.

1957 was an historic year when the company was acquired by Senior Engineering Group Limited. At the time, Seniors were seeking diversification, and decided that the air conditioning market offered the required growth potential. In 1957 the first major

contract for the newly formed organisation was secured and this proved to be critical. The work involved supplying the ductwork for the new Shell Centre on the South Bank in London - at the time this was the largest complex of its type in Europe. The work lasted five years and was worth £500,000 and got the company off to a flying start as far as its work in the south of England was concerned. In 1958 Harry Hargreaves died at the age of 80 and in 1959 the remaining buildings used by the California Engineering Company were acquired and refurbished. The effect of this acquisition was that the company had moved from small time 'tin bashing' to the field of mechanical and civil engineering, associated primarily with the air conditioning sector.

Expansion

In 1963 Hargreaves opened their plastics division and buildings were leased on York Street from Bury Corporation. The manufacture of PVC piping and ducting added a further wing to Hargreaves.

At the beginning of 1968 Hargreaves acquired further space by purchasing land formerly owned by Thwaites Brewery, and this department was converted for specialising in spiral products.

Further expansion took place after the organisation acquired the whole of the land and buildings immediately opposite their main offices and works in Lord Street from the G.E.C/ A.E.I company.

Today Senior Hargreaves is the UK's leading ductwork contractor with the capacity to produce more

This picture from 1954 was taken at a Leicestershire coal mine. The van shows how huge the mine ventilation shaft was. Indeed, it was the largest of its time and supplied by Hargreaves.

than 4000 tons of ductwork per year from the 250,000 sq ft factory in Bury. The highly skilled teams are capable of simultaneously fulfiling several multi-million pound contracts.

The Company are pioneers in all aspects of of air transfer technology. Computer aided design has revolutionised the way that systems are designed, and the latest techniques for planning and production ensure reliable delivery times.

Unrivalled expertise and resources complete the picture to ensure that Senior Hargreaves will maintain its premier position in the field of air technology.

Holcolmbe Mill - paper making in Ramsbottom for almost a century and a half

The Holcombe paper mill at Ramsbottom has been associated with papermaking in the area for 140 years. The mill was established as a paper making operation in 1857 and is therefore set to clock up a century and a half in the industry in the near future. The mill stands by the Railway Station near to the centre of the town, and close to the bridge that straddles the River Irwell. It is known that paper making began at Holcombe Mill under the ownership of J.B. Ingham and Son. From the earliest records available it is clear that casings and wrappings were made there from old bagging, jute and manilla ropes.

As the firm developed, wood pulp began to be used, along with esparto straw and new rags for making better quality paper. The late nineteenth century was a turbulent time for many companies involved in paper making, but the Mill at Holcombe survived, probably as a consequence of a policy of employing the most modern equipment available; many others were not so lucky. A trade directory from the time listed the goods produced at Holcombe Mill as 'White and Coloured Printings, Coloured Casings, Fancy Cover Papers and Small Hands'. Continuous shift working was the order of the day for employees at the mill at this time, and the rota was an exhausting

12 hour days and 12 hour nights. At the time of the annual August holiday the company gave each member of staff one day's holiday pay as a gift, quite unusual at the time.

By 1908 the company was considering plans for the future and debating the possibility of expanding production within the constraints of the water supply and effluent disposal problems. It was at this time that the adjacent cricket field was offered to the company for the very reasonable price of £6,000. The offer was turned down, eventually, though the Ramsbottom Cricket club still plays from the ground in the shadow of the mill to this day.

The 1920s, with their accompanying recession proved to be difficult for everyone concerned with paper making. This was compounded by the General Strike and the Coal Dispute of 1926; production at the mill was irregular as a result of the uncertain delivery of

with the Local Authority to support the re-introduction of the steam railway and in the landscaping of derelict land on the River Irwell. These are exciting times for Danisco Paper. Substantial investment will place them in an excellent position to take advantage of the growing demand for their quality products. And the firm's promise to be good neighbours will ensure that the harmonious partnership with the local community will continue for many years to come.

Facing page, far left: A letterhead dating from 1930 when the company was still known as Ramsbottom Paper Mill.
Facing page, right: This picture dates from the turn of the century, and shows the mill, including five mill chimneys.
Left: A flood in the 1960s caused devastation in the locality. This picture shows the river Irwell looking North from the entrance of Holcolmbe Mill.
Below: An aerial view of the mill taken in the 1990s.

coal, which carried a high premium when supplies did get through. Another testing time for the business, but the company survived, unlike so many of its rivals at the time.

Better times for the paper industry as a whole were heralded by the end of the Second World War. These lasted until the dawn of the 1960s, when tough foreign competition brought increased challenges to the Ramsbottom paper makers. After several challenging years the company was bought out by a regional newspaper publishing group, The Liverpool Daily Post and Echo Ltd. in 1964.

Investment at the plant included a computer controlled operating system in the early 1970s which brought state of the art paper making to Ramsbottom. The company enjoyed success in several spheres, including an unrivalled run of success in the area of safety, winning the British Safety Council's top award for eight years in succession.

In 1992 the company was taken over by Danisco A/S., the huge foods-to-packaging group. Since then the firm has invested millions of pounds in its Lancashire operations. Much of the new plant is designed with the aim of improving quality, rather than increasing total production.

At Ramsbottom the company has worked closely

A story of solid fuel success that began way back in 1907...

1997 marks the 90th anniversary of the business established by Arthur Gardner in 1907, when coal provided the only means of heating the home, supplying hot water and cooking for the majority of households.

Initially, the business was run from premises in Oram Street, in the Walmersley area of Bury, and Arthur employed two carters who plied their trade from horse-drawn carts. A story is told of how Arthur Gardner, a keen supporter of the temperance movement, once stood in on the delivery round of one of his carters. On passing one local public house he was surprised to see that the horse would not pass the establishment until Arthur had gone in and out of the pub door. Even worse, the same thing happened on the return journey! Needless to say, the tee-total Arthur wasted little time in suggesting that his driver should seek out a more broadminded employer. Later, horses were superseded by a motorised deliv-

ery vehicle which was acquired in the early 1930s. Around this time, Harry Snape joined the firm and worked alongside Arthur until the outbreak of the Second World War when he was called to active service. Sadly, Arthur died whilst Harry was serving in the army, and, as the supply of coal was a reserved occupation, Harry was re-called to run the business.

Harry, and his wife Marion, who still has an interest in the company, purchased the business from Arthur's widow, paying her seven shillings and sixpence per week for life, along with a weekly bag of coal and a cooked chicken at Christmas. Harry's young sons would often deliver coal on a bogey when icy conditions prevented the horses from climbing the steeper slopes about the town.

This evidently gave the boys a taste for the business, as following incorporation in 1958, Harry's elder son Chris joined the company. His younger brother Peter followed in 1967, and together the two brothers took on responsibility for the running of the business following Harry's death in 1978.

sales to industry and the public service sector increased. This necessitated the purchase of heavy goods vehicles of various types to accommodate the individual delivery requirements of each customer. It was decided to establish a sister company to deal with the haulage side of the business and Oram Street Transport Ltd seemed a natural choice of name.

With 90 years in business already 'in the bag', the directors of Gardners are well placed to see the firm clock up its first century in business. Arthur Gardner really would have been proud.

Facing page, far left: Arthur Gardner (centre) outside the office around 1920.
Facing page, right: A carter with an early example of the firm's transportation.
Left: Petrol driven open backed trucks revolutionised the solid fuel business. This sturdy example dates from around 50 years ago.
Below: Gardners rolling stock in use on the East Lancs Railway Bury to Rawtenstall line.

A third generation of the Snape family, Chris's son Gary and daughter Sallie are now actively involved in the business, and if his two grandsons, Christopher and Harry (named after his great-grandfather) follow in his footsteps, the Snape family could be running the business for many years to come.

In the 90 years since its inception, Gardner's has seen many changes. Numerous acquisitions over the years have resulted in A Gardner (Bury) Ltd becoming one of the largest privately owned solid fuel wholesalers and retailers in the country.

Coal sales grew from 1500 tons per year to 3000 tonnes per week. As the business grew it became necessary to move to larger premises, and Oram Street was vacated in favour of two depots, one at Buckley Wells in Bury, and a second in Heywood at the goods yard of Heywood Railway Station.

A further move to Prettywood at Heap Bridge followed, before the present depot at Bury Bridge was established in 1982.

As the demand for domestic coal lessened due to customers converting to gas and electricity, so the

Engraving excellence in Bury for over 150 years

The history of JSH, the trading style of John Spencer (Hazelhurst) Limited, can be traced back over a century and a half to the 1840s. Visitors to the Bolton Road West works of the company will notice the sign proclaiming the nature of business undertaken by the company; 'John Spencer (Hazelhurst) Ltd - Engraving Technology for over 150 years'. John Spencer, the founder of the firm and the man referred to in the sign, was mentioned in the census of 1851; he lived in the building which is now occupied by the present business premises, and was aged 28 when the census information was recorded. John Spencer's occupation was listed as 'engraver', and he was born at Ringley. In the later census of 1861 he was described as a 'Master Engraver employing 16 men and 5 boys'. John Spencer was married to Alice, and the couple had four children. During this period there was a concentration of engravers around the Hazelhurst area. It was not uncommon for people in a particular trade to gather in one locality in the nineteenth century. This might have been due to the availability of raw materials, some other natural resource (such as water), or the availability of skilled or specialist labour.

Calico

The early business was mainly concerned with printing a design on calico, a type of cotton cloth. The method of achieving the pattern on the material involved carving the design on a wooden block and then pressing the block, with the appropriate dye upon it, against the cloth.

This method was effective but slow, and required the careful matching of each imprint as the piece of cloth was worked upon. As the textile industry gathered momentum and the demand for patterned cloth grew, it became clear that the traditional methods of printing designs on cloth could simply not keep pace. The solution to the dilemma came in the form of roller printing. This method involved the engraving of the pattern onto a small roller (a die), initially a steel rod of about 3/4" circumference. This master pattern was then transferred by means of a 'mill' onto the final roller which would come into contact with the cloth. The John Spencer's works at Hazelhurst was using this method of *mill engraving* by 1880, a fact confirmed by the existence of original samples of

cloth retained by the company to this day. Several other reminders of the past remain within the possession of the company today, including pieces of engraving machinery which date back to the 1880s. The era of mill engraving lasted for over a century, finally coming to an end in 1988. Computer power has now replaced some of the skills that helped the

the manufacture of wallpaper, textiles and a whole host of other printing applications.

First in Britain

The year 1988 saw the acquisition of a very special laser engraving system, the first of its kind in the UK. This represented a major investment for the company and has helped John Spencer Ltd keep ahead of the field, despite intense competition from overseas. Foreign competition is a constant concern at the company, and the challenge is met head on by taking the battle abroad in the form of a continuous export drive. The company is now managed by the fifth generation of the Forshaw family and each generation has invested heavily in new machinery and skilled craftsmen. This has enabled the company to provide first class levels of service to its customers and keep one step ahead of the competition. The founder, John Spencer really would have been be proud.

firm prosper for 150 years, but the careful attention to detail and drive for increasing levels of quality and efficiency that have characterised the business from its earliest days, remain intact.

Descendant

Modern technology is just a part of the plethora of developments at Spencer's which have resulted in them achieving a reputation as a world leader in the field of laser engraving of rotary printing screens.

The current managing director, John Forshaw, is a direct descendant of the founder of the firm and is proud of the way that the company has adopted modern methods so successfully. The company is recognised as engravers of the finest quality rotary printing screens, used in

Above: Before the onset of motorisation, horses were used for transporting goods. This picture dating from the last century shows some of the 'fleet' used by JSH. *Facing page, left:* John Forshaw pictured with his wife, Amelia (daughter of the founder of the company) in the late 1800s. *Facing page, right:* This photograph shows the original workforce, taken in the 1860s. John Forshaw is pictured third row back, second from the right. John Spencer (founder of the company) can be seen third from the left in the bowler hat. *Top left:* Taken in the 1880s, this picture shows the original premises of JSH. A member of the family, William Forshaw can be seen in the doorway. *Left:* A turn of the century picture showing the workforce. John Spencer is in the centre row, fifth from the right.

Above: This imposing picture shows the Royal Cinema in 1954. The building began life as the Theatre Royal, indeed it was once described as the most popular theatre in the north of England. Some of the biggest 'names' performed here, including Sir Henry Irvine and George Eliot, not to mention Charlie Chaplin and Fred Karno's Circus. It was opened as a theatre in 1889 and served the people of Bury as a centre of excellence in the field of Pantomime, Variety and Drama for over 40 years. Then came an upsurge in the popularity of cinema. The Scala showed the first talking picture in Bury in 1929. The writing was on the wall, and four years later the Royal proudly began showing films too. Later the ornate exterior which had characterised the building for many decades was given a facelift. The result is shown here, a rather bland, almost Art-Deco style with clean, simple lines which characterised the modern age of entertainment.

Mystery surrounds the reason this photograph was taken; Above the words 'Woman's World' is a promotional 'can' of *Heinz Strained Foods.* Furthermore, the people in the picture are mainly women, and they are more interested in facing the camera than queuing to enter the cinema. Was this a Heinz exhibition of some kind we wonder? Please write and let us know if you can!

Left: The Admiral Lord Nelson Hotel (one of thousands around Britain named after her most accomplished Sea Lord) was situated a stone's throw from Bolton Street Railway Station at 29 Bolton Street, Bury. This photograph was taken in 1965 and features the Palais (or Palais de-Dance as the more mature among us would have known it) the former cinema and roller skating rink. Countless Bury couples met and did their courting here. Tales are told about the owners' policy in the Teddy-Boy Era when the management put up sign which read 'Youths in Edwardian Dress Not Admitted'. Was this, perhaps a modern day example of the King Canute syndrome? - or a clever ploy to provide a safe haven for people worried about the Teddy Boy craze and the violence which sometimes went with it? After sterling service as a picture house the Palais' fortunes were rejuvenated when it was turned into a dance hall in 1939, a run followed which lasted into the 'sixties, through 1964 when it celebrated it's 25th year in this form. Sadly the run was to end in the flames of a devastating fire which destroyed the building in 1970.

Below: The Royal Cinema from a different angle, looking towards Back Georgiana Street. The long shadows and the virtually deserted streets suggest that the picture was taken in the early evening.

Above: A 1951 photograph showing the Art Cinema and Cafe. The building on Haymarket Street remains strikingly similar in appearance, almost 50 years later. Here we see a couple walking into the advance booking office. There are advertising signs about the place for the 'Elusive Pimpernel' and for Joan Crawford in 'Harriet Craig'. There are several notices promoting the catering services offered in the Art Cafe itself. Eating out in the years after the war must have been a novelty for many local people. Many readers of this book will be of an age where they can remember the highly popular Saturday morning matinees at the Art Cinema. The behaviour of the children is variously described as riotous and unruly; visions of St. Trinian's spring to mind, with excitable youngsters exchanging a variety of missiles and using the once-plush upholstered seats for cover as the frustrated cinema staff fought to retain control. It is said that order was always restored as soon as the lights went down to indicate the start of the feature. Happy days!

Below: This imposing photograph shows the impressive Whitehead clock tower which has stood on this site since 1914. The tower was built on the site of a privately-owned lunatic asylum and was a gift to the people of Bury from Henry Whitehead, in the memory of his brother, the famous surgeon, Walter Whitehead. The Whitehead family were related to John Kay, the inventor of the *flying shuttle* which revolutionised the textile industry. Another famous Whitehead, Robert, was the inventor of the torpedo. Same shape, different function.

Above: This tranquil scene depicts a view towards the 'Bury Shopping Centre' along Haymarket Street, and dates from 1958. The optimistically-named shopping centre was constructed before the start of the Second World War, after a fire in 1933 destroyed a large part of the block which stood on the site. The fire began in the premises of Thomas E Mansergh Ltd, the well-known Millers in Bury, and quickly spread out of control watched by crowds standing in nearby Kay Gardens. On the right of the shopping centre the popular Raven Hotel and Rayner's Vaults can be seen in this picture. Other commercial premises include the Colson Milk Bar and Sam Fletcher's high class Gents Outfitters. On the far right the spire of Bury Parish Church is shown peeping over the rooftops.

Right: Travelling fairground companies were always popular when they stopped off at Bury for a few days to entertain the youthful. Of course, they still tour the country, and most young people today will have experienced the questionable pleasures of the Big Wheel, the Waltzer, the Dodgems and the Shooting Gallery. The major difference, however, between the fairground visit of today and the same trip undertaken forty or fifty years ago, is not what happens at the fairground, it's what happens away from it. Modern youngsters have endless sources of entertainment and amusement, not least of which being the television, home computers, burger bars and amusement arcades. True, there was a cinema on every street corner in *our day*, but the week the fair came to town was a very special occasion. Most of us will remember passing the milestone when we were allowed us to visit the Fair on our own or with friends. How our parents must have worried!

Left: Just over thirty members of staff from *Ringmill's* about to set off on a day trip. The date on the back of the photograph was 1947, so the scene reflects a moment in history just after the Second World War. The ladies look well wrapped-up, and understandably so if the wet cobble stones underfoot are an indication of the weather in store for them. Notice the wide collars on the day trippers coats, entirely typical for the time. Keen eyes may just be able to spot one or two men standing at the rear of the group. They were obviously in for a treat on the day, spending it as they would with 30 excitable, giggling women. Little did they realise that over half a century later their photograph would be published in a book about Bury for their grandchildren to see!

Left: The custom of Whit Walks goes back to the beginning of the nineteenth century in Manchester, when children would gather on St. Anne's Square to take part in a Whitsuntide church service. The practice spread to neighbouring towns. It was abandoned in the mid 1960s when Spring Bank Holiday replaced the Friday as the public holiday. The ladies pictured here are members of St. Joseph's Church, and they are seen enjoying the sunshine on their walk in 1953.

Looking through the old copies of the 'Bury Times' in the library, as we did in the preparation of this book, one is struck by the advertisements in the paper for ladies and children's frocks in the couple of weeks before the holiday. Lewis's of Manchester would take a quarter of a page to describe their frocks, all intended to show off mother and daughter to the best advantage in this important social event.

Right: This photograph dates from about 1953. Many younger people reading this book may be surprised to see that Bury once had a cycle track located at the end of Alfred Street, in the shadow of the mighty Pilot Mill. Cycling was very popular in the 1950s. Car ownership was still way beyond the reach of most ordinary working folk, and a cycle, followed perhaps by a motorcycle in due course, would have represented some welcome independence on the transport front. Cycling holidays were commonplace, cycling clubs were well supported, and it was only natural that the enthusiasm for two-wheeled pedal-power would result in the demand for organised racing. This demand, as confirmed by this picture, was as strong from spectators as it was from the athletes themselves. Bury's banked cycle track did not stand the test of time however, and closed a few years later.

Right: April 21 1900, and Bury Football Club has reached the F.A Cup Final just 15 years after being formed. The game was played at the Crystal Palace ground in London in front of a crowd of 68,945, and First Division Bury romped home 4-0 winners against Southampton from the Southern League. James McLuckie scored after 9 and 13 minutes, William Wood made it 3-0 after 16 minutes, and Jack Plant finished the scoring ten minutes from time as Bury became easy victors.

Here, The Shakers are on the attack, with a throw-in being taken just inside the Southampton half of the field. Interestingly, the players do not yet have any numbering system on the backs of their shirts, and the referees and linesmen are kiited-out in full suits and caps!

Left: February 23 1901, and F.A Cup holders Bury continue their defence of the trophy with a second-round visit to non-league Tottenham Hotspur, having already beaten Sheffield Wednesday 1-0 away from home in round one. Despite the boost of a Jaspen - McLuckie goal after three minutes, The Shakers were to lose 2-1 against the Southern League team, and were eliminated from the competition. They perhaps gained a little consolation from the fact that Spurs went on to win the F.A Cup - the only time ever that a non-league team has won the trophy! In this photograph Spurs keeper Clawley fists out a shot from Bury's outside-left Jack Plant (far right) to help them retain their lead. Notice that the players 'knickers' as they were referred to, come a couple of inches below the knee, whilst the Spurs keeper is wearing the same striped shirt as the outfield players - confusing!

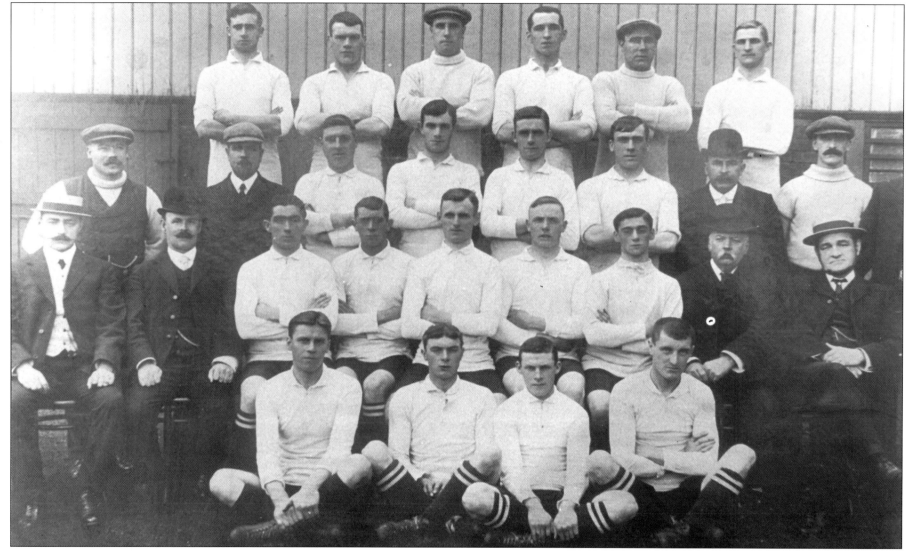

There are no smiles to be seen anywhere in this 1908/9 photograph of Bury Football Club's players, officials and directors, and there was little to smile about for the Shakers in this particular season as the club battled for the fifth time in six years against relegation from Division One. The Shakers eventually finished in 17th position (out of 18 clubs) with 36 points from their 38 games, but, thankfully only the bottom team was relegated in this early part of the 20th century. Bury's big star at this time was Billy Hibbert (featured second from the left on the front row) and he scored 26 goals from 38 games in 1908/9. He was destined for bigger and better things with Newcastle United a few years later.

Pictured are, (back row): Gill, Lindsay, Morris, McMahon, Raeside, Booth. (middle row) Miles (Trainer), Hamer (Secretary), Bigden, Currie, Rae, Humphries, Brown (Director), Yates (Trainer), Ashworth (Director) (front row) Montgomery (Manager), Horrocks, Gildea, Lindley, Pearson, Kay, Day, Unsworth (Director) Duckworth (Director) (on the ground) Turnell, Hibbert, Gibson, Broome.

Drama at Gigg Lane on 18 October 1947 as Shakers keeper George Bradshaw is stretchered off the field after breaking his right leg in an 8th minute challenge with a Newcastle United player. He is seen here being carried off the field by numerous St. John Ambulencemen as several concerned players look on. The Bury players pictured from right to left are Bill Griffiths, Don Carter (who scored a hat-trick in this game which Bury eventually lost 3-5) and Reg Halton. Centre-forward Jimmy Constantine went in goal for Bury but was unable to prevent a decisive Newcastle win. The old South Stand and Paddock on the far side of the ground are clearly packed, as the game attracted a crowd of 23,827.

Left: Bury players line up for the annual photo-call session just prior to one of the Shakers home games early in the 1949/50 season. The post-war football team saw attendances at Gigg Lane nudging towards 20,000 at times but the Shakers struggle against relegation from Division Two, and eventually finish in eighteenth position, with just fourteen wins from their 42 games. Bury's top scorer is Dave Massart who grabbed 16 league goals for the club, but there were to be many more battles ahead for the Shakers in the 1950s.

Pictured are: Back row: Whitworth, W.Griffiths, Clegg, Bardsley, G.Griffiths, Fairclough.

Front: Hazlett, Worthington, Massart, Bodle, Barclay.

Right: Oh the joy of being a football fan and seeing your team win! The emotion which is created at a football match, the pride of a winning team and the great sense of identity and achievement which a town can gain from its football club is clearly illustrated in this photograph from 26 January 1980.

The occasion is an F.A Cup Fourth Round tie at Gigg Lane against local rivals Burnley, and the Third Division Shakers have just knocked out higher division Burnley 1-0 thanks to a goal from Alan Whitehead in front of a massive crowd of 17,722. A tantalising 5th round visit to play Liverpool at Anfield was in prospect, and these young boys who ran onto the pitch to congratulate their heroes would be desperate to see that game!

This picture, dating from 1951 shows The Rock and the newsagents on the corner of Butcher Lane. The buildings here appear very grimy in this, the time before smoke free zones and relatively car-free town centres. The newsagents featured here has a good display of posters advertising many newspapers familiar to the readers of today - and some, including 'John Bull' and 'Picture Post' which are only memories to most of us. Some readers may be surprised by the advert on the side of the building for Heinz spaghetti; this scene was captured only six years after the end of the war and it is likely that people had been conditioned into being a little more adventurous about what they would eat.

Left: A view of The Rock taken almost half a century ago in 1951. The building featured in the centre of the picture is the Stanley Arms, and the faint notice on the side of the building advertises the beer sold on the premises, supplied by Walker and Homfreys. The double decker bus approaching the camera was operated by the Ribble Bus Company.

The early 1950s were difficult times for many people. War time shortages still applied to many of the products we now take for granted. Things which were available, particularly so-called luxury goods, were expensive. Living conditions were tough for many Bury residents, with inside lavatories and bathrooms being the things dreams were made of for many folk, living in damp, overcrowded conditions. Things would get better, but it would take another decade before real benefits would start to be felt.

Right: A delightful picture of Union Street, one of the roads leading off The Rock, as it was nearly half a century ago, in 1951. The curvaceous motor-cars bring back memories of the 1950s. Judging by the direction in which some of them are parked, it is clear that this scene dates from a few years before the street was made 'one-way'.

In this view the camera is pointed in the direction of The Rock, and the familiar landmark, Downham's Ironmongery and Furnishers is the building on the right, just beside the characterful Bedford lorry. At this time The Rock was beginning to attract national retail chains to Bury, such was the expansion of retailing and the attraction of the compact and highly focussed shopping area.

Another view of Union Street, this time from 1963 and featuring Bury Brewery's Pineapple Inn, a popular back-street watering hole among serious drinkers. The year that this picture was taken, 1963, is worth a special mention, for it was by far the most dramatic of the decade. Towering above all the events of the *sixties* was the assasination of John F. Kennedy, followed a few days later by the very public murder of the man accused of the act. Closer to home, the 'Profumo affair' rocked Britain causing the resignation of the Minister at the heart of the scandal after he admitted a relationship with Christine Keeler. 1963 was also the year of the Great Train Robbery, when daring thieves stole £1million from a Post Office mail train. Royalists flinched when a youthful Prince Charles was spotted drinking cherry brandy on a school trip.

Below: Looking at this photograph from the late 1950s reminds us of just how many small retail establishments used to line this popular shopping street. The shop on the left, just visible in the picture, was Dunn and Co. - hat makers and tailors according to their fascia board. Other well-known names include Loyds the radio, television and cycle shop, Martins the fashion shop, Janet-Louise fashions, and the large vertical sign half way along the street belonged to Woodhouses. People may recall these distinctive street lights, suspended by wires along this section of the roadway.

Left: A familiar view of The Rock, with Hornby Buildings on the right hand side of the picture, and shops decked out with sun shades to protect their wares from the intensity of the summer sun. Much has been written about The Rock over the years. And understandably so too, as the area has been the focal point of established retail activity in Bury for over a century. Before the advent of pedestrianisation, this was the main arterial road through the centre of the town and The Rock, as we know it today, was made up of four different streets; Fleet Street, Rock Street, Water Street, and Stanley Street. In the early years of Bury's town centre development, the narrowness of the road resulted in major congestion, with a frustrating state of affairs for motorists, retailers and shoppers alike. Road widening took place in the 1930s, and the section of The Rock seen here was the subject of attention when Hornby Buildings was constructed in 1933. Soon afterwards, in 1936, Fleet Street and Stanley Street became known as The Rock. Modern shoppers can take advantage of a stroll along the now car-free section of this once-choked shopping street, and reflect occasionally on the many changes which have taken place here over the years.

An interesting view of The Rock which dates from 1958. The one-way street on the right of the photograph which joins The Rock is Union Street, and the bank on the right is William Deacons Bank Ltd. The very distinctive building in the centre of the scene was occupied by Downhams, the well-known ironmongery business which had been founded a century before this picture was taken. In 1971 the property was demolished to make way for further pedestrianisation. Other familiar retailers along this section of the street included Van Allen and Alexander the tailors.

Another section of The Rock, this time with the corner of Crompton Street on the right of the picture. This corner was well known and very popular as a consequence of Timothy Whites Chemists being situated here. Slightly further down The Rock, *The Hand and Shears* public house was located, and past that 'Timpsons' and William Deacons Bank can be seen. On the left, the large dark building which housed Downhams the ironmongers and mill furnishers is clearly in view. The rear of a motor car parked on Crompton Street is a little deceptive to anyone trying to 'date' the photo. The vehicle probably dates from the 1930s, at least 20 years before this picture was taken.

Right: The Rock as it was in the 'swinging sixties' and seen in this view recorded in 1964. Saxone, Lacey's and True Form are shop names which may rekindle a memory or two, located in this picture on the left of the street near the zebra crossing. The sombre-faced Luton-bodied lorry approaching the camera adds a little atmosphere to the picture; you can almost hear the whining gearbox and the crunching gear changes as it makes its way along the street.

Looking at pictures of familiar streets, even from such a short period of around forty years ago, is almost guaranteed to bring back memories of shopping trips and the familiar faces of the shop-keepers we would routinely visit each week. Shopping was more more of a personal, even social activity in those days. It is also surprising how we used to manage on the narrow footpaths in town in the days before pedestrianisation.

Left: Union Square is known to date from at least 1784, when reports from the time describe how a local man, Richard Howarth, laid a foundation stone for the first building. Later, Richard Howarth was the first Bury man to acquire a printing press, after making his money selling books. The area was once a very up-market residential location in Bury, the home of important mill-owners, professional people and civic leaders. It was known, in relatively recent times as the home of Casewell's, the internationally renowned black pudding manufacturer, which operated from nearby Spring Street.

Wartime Bury saw the Square dug up to accommodate massive air-raid shelters in 1939; cast in concrete, they were capable of taking around 700 people in the event of a Nazi air-raid.

Union Square had a more pleasant use, for it was here that thousands of people would meet for the Whitsuntide processions, held annually by local churches. Sadly, when the town-centre redevelopment of the 1960s took place, the area was cleared to make way for a modern shopping centre.

Left: Another view of the Market Place. The grime on the building housing the Ribble booking office and the Blackburn Assurance Co. (sometimes known as Castle Chambers) is also present on the statue of Sir Robert Peel. The statue is, without doubt, the central feature in this, the heart of Bury. Peel died in 1850 after being thrown from his horse in Hyde Park. It was bought through public subscription, in 1852, two years after the death of the famous politician. It is known that 20,000 people turned out to witness the unveiling of the statue which had cost £2,500 raised by 2,000 local folk. Controversy followed when it was realised that four of the statue's waistcoat buttons were fastened on the wrong side. Note the railings next to the statue which marked the location of the gents toilets located deep underground on this spot.

Right: Market Place appeared much larger in this view from 1954 than it does today. In the centre of the picture the Clarence Hotel, with its beautiful victorian gothic architecture, looks out towards the statue of Sir Robert Peel. Notice how Peel's statue is stained black with the soot and grime caused by the polluted air which had blighted every northern town since the Industrial Revolution. A twelve year smoke-control plan was drawn up in Bury about five years after this scene was recorded. It met with limited success initially, but in more recent times the air we breath and the buildings we use have benefited from the effects of enforceable pollution laws. Market Place has been the centre of Bury for almost as long as the town has existed; in early times this was the site of the sun dial, the stocks and the pillory, along with the Market Cross. The dominant building here has, of course, always been the Parish Church, though the present fine structure is about the fourth one to stand on this site. It dates from the 1870s and its construction was master-minded by the Rector of the day, Edward Geoffrey Hornby. The design incorporated the spire from the previous building and the cost of the church amounted to £27,000.

The Bury HQ of Lloyds Bank can be seen to the right of the Clarence Hotel in a building originally occupied by Driffield Bros. (drapers). Ribble, the bus operator, used to have a booking office here, based in the former entrance to the stable yards at the rear of the property. For many years the haed office of the Manchester, Bury, Rochdale and Oldham Steam Tramway Company was located here too.

A congested, and highly typical scene from 1958. The area is unmistakably Market Place. The patch of grass on the right of the picture has hardly changed over the years, it belongs, of course, to the Parish Church. The large dark building on the left of the picture is Derby Chambers. Keen eyes may make out the sign relating to Burney's the bread and cake shop, and the Elsinore Restaurant and Cafe in the distance. The Clarence Hotel, built over a ten year period between 1880 and 1890 can be seen in all its mock gothic splendour in the centre of the scene. It is particularly pleasing to see the queue of modest family saloon cars shown here, like some modern classic car event or a clip from an old British film. Pure nostalgia!

Left: This view of Silver Street dates from 1964 and is interesting for a number of reasons. The vast majority of the fabric of the street remains as it was when the photograph was taken, including the subtle, but important fact that the street had the same 'one-way' status in 1964 as it does today, over thirty years later. The Clarence Hotel, with its interesting victorian mock-gothic architecture hardly seems to have changed. And the Midland Bank, pictured on the left, at the time of writing is also reassuringly present too. Buildings in the distance have gone to make way for the Job Centre, and of course, you rarely see cars like these today!

Right: A view of Haymarket Street before the advent of the Mill Gate Shopping Centre, the construction of which caused the demolition of some of the buildings featured here. This photograph dates from 1961, the dawn of one of the most dynamic decades in recent times. In view of this it is worth mentioning the presence, in the picture of the UCP Tripe Shop, in the distant centre of the picture. It was as much an icon of Bury as the two Ford Cortinas parked here were motoring icons of 1960s Britain. The 'Swinging Sixties' are a rich source of nostalgia; a time when Society was turned upside down, and moral values changed forever.

Bury is fortunate to have this pleasant oasis in the town centre where shoppers and travellers may relax for a while and reflect on the activities of the day. The area known as Kay Gardens has a wealth of history behind it. It was once the location of the Derby Market, a retail facility with a chequered history which was provided for local traders in 1839. It struggled by until the turn of the century when it finally gave up the ghost. Few people were sad to see it go. It was around 1908 when the gardens were completed and ready for townsfolk to enjoy them. Kay Gardens were named in memory of John Kay, the inventor of the flying shuttle, by one of his descendants Henry Whitehead. Shortly after the Second World War the area around the gardens became very congested as a consequence of it being used as the starting point for most of the town's bus routes. It is said that the area was used by an estimated 40 million passengers per year. Plans to relieve the congestion in the area involved the construction of an interchange at The Mosses. This scheme was eventually discarded in favour of a new facility to be built at Knowsley Street.

Disasters!

A major disaster was averted by a quick-thinking railway employee at Bury Knowsley Street Station, in January 1952. A footbridge over the track was being crossed by 138 football supporters after a local derby match between Bury and Blackburn Rovers. The whole floor of the 75 foot long bridge dropped out onto the track below, under the weight of the fans as they trooped across the walkway, causing the unfortunate supporters to fall 25 feet onto the hard surface beneath them. This was bad enough of course, but the disaster could have been even worse had it not been for the senior porter on duty, David Foulkes; Mr Foulkes had the foresight to run to the signal box to warn a speeding oncoming train to stop. He was just in time, and the train halted just 200 yards short of the tangled, groaning heap of supporters who lay in agony on the cold January ground.

20 ambulances were called to the scene, along with firefighters and police officers. All worked tirelessly to clear the track and give first aid to the stricken fans. Off-duty medical staff were called in to work and 44 people were detained in hospital with a variety of broken bones and head injuries. The hero of the day was David Foulkes; his presence of mind prevented an even greater disaster from descending on the town of Bury.

Right: A major fire brought grief to Bury in February 1960. The location was a former cotton mill being operated by the Apex Bedding Company in Heys Street. Forty female workers became trapped on the top floor of the building and were led to safety by the 60 year old works director. The blaze took over five hours to bring under control, and a roll call of staff was conducted outside the building by the managers of the company. Tragically, it was found that two female members of staff had been trapped in the building by the raging fire and their lives were lost. Firefighters are pictured here pouring thousands of gallons of water into the stricken building.

Mill fires have been a common occurrence in many Lancashire towns over a number of years. A combination of several factors makes old mills particularly vulnerable to fire; spilt oil, used to maintain rows of tightly packed machinery, would soak into the thick timber flooring over a number of years. This, along with large quantities of dry fabric, and the ever present threat of a spark from old electrical wiring, means that the threat of fire was rarely very far away.

Left: This fire at a tyre dump in the Bury area was caught on camera by Rochdale press photographer Clifford C Ashton. It was a warm spring day when the fire broke out in 1953. The Mayor of Bury was having lunch in the vicinity of the blaze, and heard the commotion as people tried desperately to control the flames. Burning tyres always pose a challenging task for fire fighters; it is very difficult to get the water on every part of the flaming rubber, and tyres produce thick black smoke which makes the extent of the task hard to determine. Often, the only way to make an impact on a blaze like this is to knuckle down and move tyres out of the way, before they too catch fire. As can be seen here, dozens of people quickly volunteered to move the tyres to safety, including the Mayor of Bury who left his lunch to join the helpers. Now that's what we call leading by example!

Left: The fire which destroyed the Market Hall was the subject of many photographs when it lit up the sky in November 1968. Few, however managed to capture the atmosphere of the event as successfully as this one does; you can almost smell the smoke in the damp air and hear the cracking timbers, punctuated by occasional falls of masonry as the fire wrapped itself around its hapless victim. The droning of the diesel-driven pumps on the fire appliances filled the air on the night; there were only a handful of spectators to the blaze as firefighters calmly and quietly went about their task.

This spectacular photograph was taken by Clifford Ashton of Rochdale, well known in newspaper circles for his breathtaking images of fires and other disasters which blighted Lancashire, for a period of over 50 years. Clifford worked for many national newspapers and insurance companies over his long career, recording the devastation and sharply contrasting aftermath of events such as this one. We are grateful to Mr Ashton for allowing us to use his photographs in this book.

Right: Spectacular scenes in November 1968 when a major blaze destroyed the market hall. Misery was caused to dozens of small business people who saw their livelihoods go up in smoke on the crisp winter night. Bury folk were sad too; after all, the market had served them well for almost seventy years, and to many people it seemed like the passing of an old friend when news of the fire spread around the town on the following day. Pictures from the time show firemen confronting a seemingly hopeless situation as the smoke and flames rose over a hundred feet into the air. The council organised a temporary market hall for the town in February 1968. This was used until the new market opened in October 1971. Many Bury citizens look back on the old market hall and have fond memories of shopping trips there; the sights, sounds and smells which vanished for good in

Right and below: Utter devastation was the scene at the market, the day after the fire, as can be seen in this photograph. Visitors looked on in disbelief at the twisted remains of the once-proud building. This elevated view, framed by the early morning November mist shows the full extent of the damage; it must have been obvious to 'those in the know' that the idea of rebuilding the facility was a non-starter. There was sadness too for the scores of traders who had lost their means of earning a living in the blaze. No doubt some of them will be featured in this photograph, looking at the scene of devastation and

wondering what the future was to hold for them. The photograph above graphically highlights just how extensive the damage was. At street level the casual observer may have been forgiven for thinking that the fire had caused serious, but superficial damage, after all, the distinctive domed roof of the market hall and the shop fronts of the businesses which surrounded it all seemed to be generally intact. This slightly elevated view shows that the fire had destroyed virtually everything apart from these features, and that the idea of repairing the market could not even be considered.

This mid-1930s picture shows a 'rival' motorbus alongside the more established electric trams at Kay Gardens, the centre of much transport activity in Bury for many years. This picture is very atmospheric, with the ornate tram standards and overhead wires carrying the electric power to drive the vehicles, and the sea of granite cobble stones which characterised every northern town for decades. Other features worthy of note include the Co-Op building on the right of the picture, and the memorial to John Kay standing in Kay Gardens
At the time this photograph had been taken motorbuses had been operating on the streets of Bury for around a decade; the electric trams had been a familiar sight around the town since 1903.

Right: Guaranteed to bring back memories! Close your eyes and recall the unique aroma of damp seat fabric, tobacco smoke and varnished wood; This Leyland double decker bus pictured opposite the premises originally established by Carr's Automobile Engineers along Knowsley Street. The bus seen here is listed in a log of all the vehicles owned and operated by the Corporation's public transport department. The records shows that it is a Leyland PD1, purchased from Northern Counties which entered service in December 1946. By the time this photograph was taken, at the dawn of the 1960s, the vehicle was almost half way through its working life in Bury. EN 8813 went on to serve local people until March 1977 when it was withdrawn after 31 years and around one million miles on the highways and byways of Bury.

Left: This delightful 26-seat, single decker Guy Wolf was brought into service in Bury in July 1948. Records show that it was one of two lightweight, short wheel-base vehicles bought especially for the Nangreaves route. This vehicle was withdrawn from service in January 1955 and went on to be used as an ambulance by Bury Corporation. In 1960 it found a new home in Heywood, as a mobile shop. The bus was broken up in July 1963. Bury's first local bus routes began in 1925 with a half-hourly service from the town centre to Walshaw and Elton, travelling via Bolton Street, Croston's Road and Walshaw Road. Initially the fleet consisted only of two Leyland Motors vehicles, registration numbers EN 2630 and EN 2631 in fine vermilion and cream hand-painted livery. At the time their speed was limited 20mph.

Left: This picture was one of several taken in 1967 to mark the delivery of a batch of new public transport vehicles by Bury Corporation. In all, three Daimler single deckers were purchased, each 33 feet in length and fitted with dual entrance bodies and 41 seats. The vehicles could accommodate a further 19 passengers standing. In addition, four Leyland double-deckers were acquired, and the bodies for all the vehicles described here were built at the works of East Lancashire Coach Builders.

Some of us look back with sadness on the modernisation of bus fleets. This epitomises a characteristic of nostalgia; we all want the benefits of warmer, quieter, cleaner (in terms of pollution, at least) buses, but we miss the real 'character' of vehicles from the past. In 1969 the Council lost its independent control of the bus service as the Selnec Transport Authority was given control over all bus operations in the Manchester area.

Right: 'Carry on Camping'... for just £585 (plus car tax) a family of four could enjoy the freedom of the road, and the camp site, in this Bedford Dormobile, on sale at Auty and Lees on The Rock. A sought after classic vehicle now, the Bedford had a column gearchange, powerful petrol engine and, of course, a kitchen sink! The Vauxhall Victor would have been a popular buy too. Not many of these survive now, they had a dreadful reputation for suffering the effects of rust in the 1960s which makes surviving examples rare.

It was unusual for a town of the rather modest size of Bury to have two railway stations. Knowsley Street Station, pictured here, was built by the Manchester and Leeds Railway Company in 1848. A line from Manchester to Littleborough had been opened in 1839, and in 1841 a branch line extended the service to Heywood. When the company opened the Knowsley Street Station the service operated between Bury and Liverpool. Many readers will, no doubt, have fond memories of catching the train from Knowsley Street to the coastal resorts. This picture is one of several supplied to us by Mr E F Bentley. Knowsley Street Station received her last passenger service in October 1970 and was demolished in 1971.

Left: This delightful scene was captured one Sunday in September 1957. The location is unmistakably Bury Bolton Street Station, and features a Class 5 locomotive about to leave for Manchester Victoria via Clifton Junction. The 15.20 from Colne, a five-car Lancashire and Yorkshire Railway 1916 EMU is in the up-bay platform. It is difficult not to be moved by the sight of the powerful, dark steam engine, as it prepares to haul its train off towards Manchester. Bury is fortunate to remain one of the handful of British towns to keep a 'proper' railway complete with locomotives such as this one. The unsung heroes who fought for the facility and maintain it today should be given all the support we can muster.

It is quite amazing to think that the station featured here has been in use since 1847, a period of over one and half centuries, and reassuring that it is in such safe hands today.

Right: Trainspotters will appreciate this photograph of locomotive number 48437 as it approaches Bury Bolton Street Station, and the rest of us will be pleased to see an unusual view of this side of the town as it was in 1963. The goods train is the 17.10 Nelson-Moston class D we are told.

The Railway Age came to Bury in the years between 1840 and 1860. It is difficult, looking back, to comprehend the massive impact that railways had upon local industry and the lives of ordinary people around the town. Tremendous activity was generated which set Bury on the road to success.

Right: Locomotive number 42644 leaving Bury Bolton Street Station on its way to Bacup. On board was the Three Counties Tour which had been organised for the Manchester Rail Travel Society. The picture was taken at 11.09 on Saturday 26 November 1966.

Quite apart from the train featured here, the photograph is an interesting record of a well-known local landmark, Bury Power Station. It may seem strange to younger people that a power station should be located so close to the centre of town, particularly as these facilities produced much pollution. This, however, was entirely typical of northern towns.

Left: Awe-inspiring. The kind of photograph you might expect to see in an exhibition, or the winner in a photography competition. It was taken by Mr E F Bentley of Tottington and shows a section of the Bolton and Bury Canal near Bury Bridge. The picture was taken in 1965 and features Crompton's Paper Mill.

The canal has been filled in here now and the area, like so many in the centre of towns such as Bury, is now the site for a car park. The picture evokes memories of damp walks along the canal bank and mysterious, lumbering barges.

East Lancashire Railway- brought back to life for all to enjoy

The original East Lancashire Railway opened in 1846 and linked Manchester to Radcliffe and Bury, via Clifton Junction. The line then continued from Bury along the Rossendale Valley, passing through the village of Summerseat and the town of Ramsbottom before reaching Rawtenstall.

An extension line from Stubbins Junction (just north of Ramsbottom) to Accrington opened in 1848, whilst the Rawtenstall branch was extended in stages, reaching Bacup in 1852. The East Lancashire Railway existed as an independent railway company until 1859 when it merged with the Lancashire & Yorkshire Railway. The Lancashire & Yorkshire Railway merged with the London & North Western Railway in 1922, but just 12 months later this became part of the London Midland & Scottish Railway (LMS), and this is how it remained until nationalisation and the formation of British Railways in 1948.

The Bury to Rawtenstall line continued to carry both passenger and freight traffic until 1972 when all passenger services were withdrawn, the Rawtenstall-Bacup Section having being closed in December 1966. Freight traffic, in the form of coal trains continued until December 1980 when the line was totally closed.

In the 134 years of operation the line saw a great variety of both motive power and rolling stock from early steam engines with open cabs, to modern diesel locomotives, from commuter traffic to Wakes Week specials; all this would have come to an end in December 1980, but for the formation of the East Lancashire Railway Preservation Society in 1968.

The original aims of the Society were to operate the section of line from Stubbins Junction to Helmshore, but this did not come to fruition, so in 1972 the East Lancashire Railway moved all its rolling stock and locomotives to Bury, establishing the Bury Transport Museum in Castlecroft goods shed, adjacent to the Bury to Rawtenstall line.

In 1980 the coal traffic on the line ceased and the line finally closed. This gave the East Lancashire Railway

Opposite page: This delightful photograph dates from September 1963 and depicts a steam locomotive approaching Bolton Street Station. It is known that this was a Bury Knowsley Street to Blackpool half day excursion. Note the building on the right of the picture which was the regional headquarters of the railway company.

Left: 45642 'Boscawen' approaching the Nuttall Tunnel, Ramsbottom with the 17.10 Nelson-Moston Class D freight train, in May 1963.

Below: A day excursion to Blackpool or Morecambe via Accrington and Blackburn is seen here stopping as Summerseat in July 1961.

All the photographs featured here were kindly supplied by Mr E F Bentley of Tottington.

the chance it had been waiting for. A joint effort between the local authorities and the railway secured Derelict Land Grants valuable enough to purchase the land between Bury and Rawtenstall.

A partnership was established between the East Lancashire Railway and the Local Authorities of Bury and Rossendale, resulting in the Line reopening between Bury and Ramsbottom on July 25th 1987, before the rest of the line was reopened to to Rawtenstall in 1991.

Rochdale local authority have now joined the partnership with the plan to open an extension from Bury to Heywood which is due to be completed in about two years.

Shopping

Left: A 1960s view of Hornby Buildings, so named in honour of the Hornby family which had so much influence in the town. The impressive parade of shops was built in 1933 by the Corporation. It is a very attractive building and represented a major improvement in the layout of this part of Bury which has always been a popular area with shoppers. Reports from the time describe how the building was lit up for two weeks after it was opened, and floodlit again in 1936 to celebrate the Jubilee of King George V. It is surely a matter of relief that Hornby Buildings has survived the demolition-mens hammer and continue to grace the streets of Bury. Just a stone's throw away, the Odeon Cinema (built three years later than Hornby Buildings) has seen its popularity come and go in recent times and sadly is no longer the vibrant picture house it once was.

Right: A scene in Bury from around thirty years ago; the year was 1968 and this view has changed beyond recognition since then. Georgiana Street runs towards the left at the bottom of the picture but the scene is dominated by the Victorian dome of the market hall.

An elevated view of Kay Gardens from 1956. Many features shown here combine to rekindle fond memories of the way the area used to look. Before the age of pedestrianisation buses used to trundle past the Co-Op building, and shelters lined the triangular pathways around the immaculately-kept gardens. Looking back, life seemed to flow at a much more relaxed pace at the time that this scene was recorded. People knew, and cared about their neighbours in those days, whereas some folk today seem to know the characters in the Soap Operas better than they know the people next door! Many of the figures seen enjoying the sunshine in this picture appear to be of the older generation, though, as most of us may remember, there is evidence of how younger people would take advantage of a sit-down on the steps of the monument. The Co-Op building looks entirely in place with its proud, plain walls and mock towers. So much more attractive than the modern glass-clad version.

Left: Another view of the Market Hall in a photograph taken sometime in the early 1960s. This is, perhaps not the most attractive view of the market buildings, the combination of brickwork, stonework, slates, the large grey dome and the angles of the other sections of roof seem to sit very uncomfortably with each other from this standpoint. Still, it is all very easy for us to get fussy about the visual appeal of some of Bury's streets in days gone by. The town is blessed with some fine buildings and we should be grateful and relieved that most of them have survived threats from changing shopping habits, wartime bombing and over zealous town planners. Other towns and cities within a few miles of the centre of Bury have gone through the same challenges but without the same success. Recently we have seen the emergence of a new threat; Out-of-town shopping areas dominated by large retail organisations threaten to reduce our town centres to ghost towns, and force long-established small companies out of business. As town centres decline we can only guess at the what the future holds for our fine old buildings.

Right: A view across the gardens towards the very distinctive roof of Bury Market. The photograph was taken in 1958. Market trading is one of the earliest recorded commercial activities in Bury, as it is in most traditional English towns. Early documents show that a charter to hold a market was granted to Sir John Pilkington, the Lord of the Manor, by Henry VI in the fifteenth century, for a market to be held each Friday. Market trading took place on the Market Place until 1839 when a purpose built new market was built on the site of the present Kay Gardens. Initially the facility, which had been provided by Lord Derby, was not at all popular with market traders. Later, in 1867, a roof constructed from glass and ornate victorian ironwork was added which improved conditions inside for traders and shoppers alike. By 1900 the roof was declared unsafe, with traders being given just two hours to quit the building for fear of collapse. The building pictured here was opened in 1901 at a cost of £15,000 by the Mayor Cllr John Battersby.

Right: Looking through local directories, from the turn of the century up until the 1950s, one can find three or four different businesses operating under the name of 'Campbells'. It is difficult to know if any of these are connected; James Campbell of 162 Hornby Street was a grocer, Campbells of 143 Lever Street were furniture dealers. Adverts in The Bury Times enticed their public with the headline 'Furnish your home for as little as £1 per month' in 1935. Those were the days!

Below: It was 'Lamb Season' for the butchers business operated by E. Derby when this photograph was taken in 1926. The shop was one of seventeen which used to border the market, and, when seen here, had been operational about 25 years. Note the bunches of mint hanging up in front of the shop which would be certain to make any self-respecting sheep go faint at the very thought of mint sauce. Notice also the lady pictured second from the left in the picture; judging by the way her hair is standing on end we can only assume that she had recently had a very nasty shock! All in all a lovely scene of day to day life from over seventy years ago.

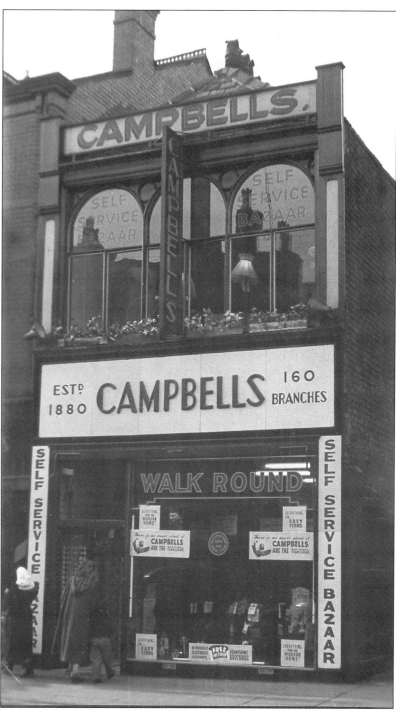

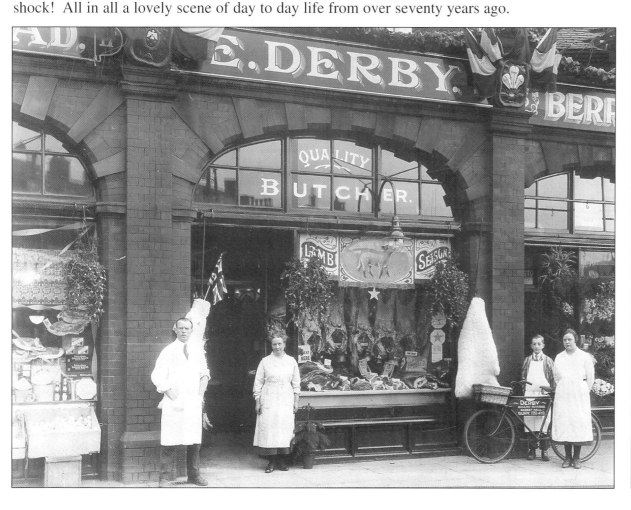

Visiting markets has been part of life in Bury for at least 500 years. Originally, markets were held on specific days for three reasons. Firstly, it allowed the people involved in growing produce and making the goods sold at the market to set aside a regular day to do the 'selling' part of their business. This had the obvious benefit of enabling them to spend the rest of the week doing the 'production' side of making their living. In the earliest days of market trading there was another reason for having the market on a particular day; it allowed merchants to travel to the market *together* as security in those days was a very real problem for anyone travelling with valuable goods or currency. Finally, lets not forget the convenience of a weekly market for citizens, all eager to buy a bargain!

Anyone who ever walked around the stalls in the open market will be drawn to this picture and reminded of the unique aromas, sights and sounds which characterised the place. This view of the Moss Street side of the open market dates from the middle of the 1960s and shows the roof of the main market building in the background. Bury's market has attracted shoppers and bargain-hunters from a much wider area than simply Bury alone, and this has been of considerable benefit to the town. During the present century the market was held on Saturdays only up until 1947 when Wednesday was included, and later, in 1953 when Friday was added. Over the years shoppers and market traders built up relationships which would have been the envy of the modern marketing men and their 'loyalty schemes'.

An elevated view over the heads of shoppers in the open market which dates from 1968. The people featured here are unaware of the photographer's lens which managed to capture the view for us to see today. It is interesting to reflect upon the issues of 1968 which would have occupied the minds of these people; It was the year that, in the United States, Robert Kennedy, was assasinated by an extremist. Martin Luther King, the popular civil rights leader met the same fate and his assassin was captured in London before being deported back to the USA to face trial. Decimalisation came into force, bound to be of great interest to the traders here, and plans were announced to reduce the voting age to18.

This roof-top view was captured in 1968 and records how this part of town looked before the market hall fire which resulted in major changes to the appearance of the area. The open market area is in the foreground and judging by the crowds around the stalls, this is clearly a market day. The building housing the covered market is in the centre of the view and this would have been one of the last quality photographs of the building before it was destroyed. The white flat walls of the Co-Op Emporium are behind the market, and the top of the Queens Hotel can be seen on the right of that. Small shops now occupy the unusual curved building, with their shop-fronts looking out towards the 'new' interchange.

Below: Bury's success over many centuries in attracting shoppers to its markets from a wide area has already been mentioned. Likewise, the changes which seen the market move from the area alongside the Parish Church to Lord Derby's Market, and then to the ill-fated building of 1901 are well known to people interested in the history of the town.

Understandably, we tend to take modern structures for granted, and look back on the buildings from the past through rose tinted spectacles, for that is the nature of nostalgia - and what makes it such a sentimental subject.

The modern market hall pictured below is like no other building featured in this book; its modern glass and concrete styling with bold gull-wings may not be to everyone's taste, but it carries out its function well and provides an efficient location for Bury's modern-day market trading activity. What will nostalgia books make of it in another 100 years, we wonder?

Above: 'Danger - men at work' may be the caption to accompany this picture and encapsulate the feelings associated with many similar scenes from the town centre during the 1960s and 1970s. A twenty-year period saw monumental changes to the shape, appearance and atmosphere of Bury. Changes which swept through the whole of the Britain, largely brought about by the need to improve the traffic flow through our towns, and the perceived need to separate 'people' from 'cars' in our town centres.

Bury Reference & Information Services

Local history

Local history materials relating to the whole Borough are located at Reference & Information Services in Bury Central Library. Materials about Radcliffe, Prestwich and Ramsbottom are kept at the libraries in those areas.

We can provide access to books and pamphlets written about the area, local newspapers, maps and photographs.

For family historians, many census and parish records are available on microfilm or microfiche at Bury Central Library - please book in advance.

We also stock a wide range of local publications for sale.

Opening hours for Bury Central Library are as follows:
Monday, Tuesday, Thursday and Friday 10am - 5.30pm.
Wednesday 10am - 7.30pm.

Leisure Services Bury Metro Libraries

Reference and Information Services, Central Library, Manchester Road, Bury, Lancashire BL9 0DG.
Telephone: 0161 253 5871
Prestwich Library: 0161 253 7216
Radcliffe Library: 0161 253 7160
Ramsbottom Library: 01706 822484

Bury Archive Service

Bury Archive Service exists to preserve those records kept by local organisations and individuals which are of permanent value, and to make them available to the public.

The Holdings date from 1675 to the present day, although most are from the late 18th to the mid 20th centuries, and range from family letters to building plans and official committee minutes.

There is material relating to all parts of the metropolitan borough.

1st Floor, Derby Hall Annexe, Edwin Street (off Crompton Street), Bury BL9 0AS
Telephone: 0161 797 6697 (answer phone outside of office hours)

The archives are open to the public from:
10am - 1pm and 2pm - 5pm each weekday.
It is necessary to make an appointment except on Tuesdays.
We are currently open on certain Saturdays
(by appointment only).
For details ring the archivist.

Bury's recycling pioneers for almost 50 years

The Brook Street Metal Company Ltd can be found nestling beside several other well known local firms in the Bridge Street area of Bury. The origins of the business go back as far as the 1950s, when it was known as 'Fargher and Heap', and some local people still refer to the company by the same name. In post-war Britain, around the time of the founding of the firm, industry was desperate for scrap metal to be used in recycling. It is hard to imagine that in those early years after the war, rationing was still in force and many of the household goods we now take for granted were in short supply. These were the days of the *Rag and Bone Man*, when the streets were 'patrolled' by these entrepreneurs with their horses and carts, eagerly collecting items of scrap metal and rags in return for a balloon or some small change. Scrap metal would be fed back to the firm's premises at Albion road, the original home of the company. Scrap metal from more traditional sources would also be recovered; the growing number of small engineering firms, agri-

cultural scrap and cars deemed too far-gone to repair. During its first decade of existence the company built a reputation for fair dealing and honesty which it has built upon to this day. This, along with shrewd business management, resulted in considerable growth until, in 1960 it was decided that the premises at Albion Street were just too small to accommodate the business any longer. It was decided to relocate, and

the search for a new site was underway. Eventually, a location which satisfied all the requirements of the company was identified and secured. This was nearly forty years ago, and the chosen site was at Bridge Street, the home of the company ever since.

A milestone in the history of the company was when Douglas Morgan was taken on in the early 1960s. Mr Morgan was a classic example of a man who learned

the job 'from the bottom upwards' and went on to become a shareholder, a director and eventually to buy the business when the opportunity arose in October 1986. Later, Mr Morgan appointed his only son, Phil to the Board of Directors, followed a few years after that by Mr Alan Ingham, a long standing employee of the firm. Further changes and appointments were to follow: in 1987, Phil Morgan's wife,

Janet joined the company, and, in 1990, their son Steven joined the rest of the family at Brook Street Metal Co. Ltd.

April 1990 was a sad time for the company. Douglas Morgan died and the running of the firm passed to his son, Phil. Phil Morgan's wife and son were appointed director/shareholders. Mr Alan Ingham remains active in the business as a director of the company.

The business, indeed the industry as a whole, has seen many changes since it was established almost half a century ago. The firm still purchases all types of Ferrous and Non-Ferrous Metals, operating a collection service for many of its customers. Any scrap metal is valued an sought after by the firm which is eager to purchase anything from Aluminium cans to old cast iron baths, and from scrap motor vehicles to complete factory clearances. A forty ton weigh-bridge on site adds to the convenience of the whole operation to the benefit of staff and customers alike.

Opposite page: Mr Douglas Morgan, pictured with one of the company's first tipper trucks in a photograph dating from the late 1950s.
Above: Modern transportation is provided by the sturdy Leyland Skip wagons.
Right: A recent view of the busy yard at Brook Street Metal Company.

Joseph Scholes - associated with the finishing trade since 1903

The name of Joseph Scholes has been associated with the Finishing Trade since 1903 when Joseph Scholes and George Garstang founded the business of Scholes and Garstang at Albert Finishing Works, Radcliffe. The partnership was dissolved in 1907 and George Garstang went into the manufacturing side with his brother in the Pioneer Mill, Radcliffe.

From then on, Joseph Scholes and his three sons, Robert, Frank and Richard carried on in the name of J Scholes and Sons. The premises were enlarged and later they acquired the Canal Works from William Beddows & Co. On April 1st 1914, they purchased the King Street Finishing Works from John Young & Co Ltd.

Later, on account of the lease at the Salford Works coming to a close, Stormer Hill Works, Tottington was purchased from the Calico Printers Association Ltd in 1918. After reorganisation the business was transferred from Salford and work commenced at Tottington in the latter part of 1919.

In 1923 a Private Limited Company under the name of Joseph Scholes & Sons Ltd was formed, the first directors being Robert Scholes, Frank Scholes and Richard Scholes.

Above: *Portland Street, Manchester taken in 1915. This picture was supplied by Joseph Scholes & Sons Limited. One of their early motorised vans can be seen on the right hand centre of the picture.*

Joseph Scholes died in 1931 and it can be said that he was held in high esteem by both his workforce and business friends alike.

Robert became chairman in that year and held this position until he died in 1942. At the same time, Richard's son Joseph was killed in the submarine 'Traveller' in the Mediterranean. Richard became chairman in 1943 and J Massey was made director.

During this year the Radcliffe works were closed, attention being focused on the Tottington Works.

When Richard died in 1947 Frank Scholes became chairman. Then in June 1948 it was agreed that Frank and his sons, Frank and William would take over the Radcliffe Works as a separate company, under the name of Joseph Scholes & Sons Limited. Robert's son, Eric was appointed chairman.

From 1953 to the 1970s and 1980s the fortunes of the company were steadily developed, manufacturing a range of furnishing fabrics for the home and export trade. The company is now solely run by Joe Scholes who has developed and expanded into specialised areas of textile finishing and engineering, with the recent acquisition of a dyeing and finishing works some three miles from the original site in Radcliffe.

Above: A memo/letterhead dating from the 1920s.

Left: The Tottington Works taken on a very windy day in the late 1800s. Keen eyes may just be able to make out the steam train behind the houses on the right and the man in a boat on the mill pond. The two men on the bank of the pond appear to have spotted the photographer and are posing for the picture.

Warburton Holgate - local engineering expertise since 1784

An aerial view of the Milltown Street works of Warburton Holgate at Radcliffe

Warburton Holgate is a locally-owned business with a world-wide reputation in its chosen field of paper, board and converting machinery for the paper industry. The Holgate side of the business has a history going back over two centuries to 1784, making it not only one of the oldest companies in the area, but one of the oldest firms in Britain.

Ship's Chandlers

The nature of the business in those days was described as 'ships' chandlers and plumbers and the company embarked on its first steps in the rapidly developing field of engineering. The company as it is organised today is the result of the merging of two well established firms, the second element being E

D Warburton which was originally formed in 1948. E D Warburton began making equipment for the paper industry in the late 1940s. The work is very specialised, and progress in recent years has been built upon the experience gained in the early years after the end of the Second World War. The company attributes much of it's success to the wealth of specialist knowledge and skills that have been built up over many decades at the firm; As Production Director Brian Rigby said 'We consider our strength lies in giving a specialist engineering and technical service to the paper industry'. The strategy appears to have worked, for Warburton Holgate has a growing list of clients, not just in this country, but as far away as Sweden, Greece, Thailand, The Philippines, Korea, Turkey, Bangladesh and India.

High quality engineering methods are employed within the company in order to keep pace with the ever increasing demands of the clients involved in the paper industry. Modern machines run at much higher speeds than was once the case, and specialist techniques have been developed at Warburton Holgate to ensure that every element of the production process, including the quality of the raw materials supplied by outside companies, is of a standard high enough to support a world-class finished product.

Tradition

Traditional skills too, are still valued at the firm which has an international reputation for its ability to refurbish and rebuild machinery, including the huge rolls used in the process, to very high standards. Several members of staff have well over 20 years experience at the firm and this is an invaluable asset when it comes to tackling some of the older equipment brought in for their attention. Brian Rigby sums up the situation quite simply; 'We need to be able to meet our customers' needs, whether they stem from technology long since considered obsolete, but in use on machines that are still turning out good quality paper, or improving on technology incorporated in some of the most modern machines in the world.' Brand new equipment is recognised as being at the cutting edge of today's technology in the paper machinery industry; the latest computer-aided design techniques combining with the experience built up over half a century resulting in a rich source of pride for everyone at the Radcliffe works of Warburton Holgate.

Press section supplied to an American company by Warburton Holgate